EVERYDAY MIRACLES

EVERYDAY MIRACLES

Poetry/Encouragement Journal

BY
REV. DENISE MARSHALL
AND LELIA L. LEWIS

XULON PRESS

Xulon Press
2301 Lucien Way #415
Maitland, FL 32751
407.339.4217
www.xulonpress.com

Unless otherwise indicated, Scripture quotations taken from the King James Version (KJV)–*public domain*.

Paperback ISBN-13: 978-1-6628-4546-8
Ebook ISBN-13: 978-1-6628-4547-5

Acknowledgments

We would like to give thanks first to
Our Lord and Savior Jesus Christ!
We thank all of our family and friends
who pray with and for us,
Our Pastors Bishop Quintin and Lady Donna Boger
Dr. Wesley and Lady Millicent Pinnock
Charles and Darlene McClendon
Our church families
Our loving staff and supporters at Word in Script
Our publishers, editors, and friends at Xulon Press
God Bless You All for who you are and all you do!

Introduction

This journal was created to encourage daily reflection
on how Wonderful God is!

If we only take the time to use our five senses seeing,
hearing, taste, smell, and touch, also we must not
forget to include our emotional sense of feeling, and
the spiritual sense of knowing.

Then we will more clearly understand, that we
encounter a special miracle every day!

Additionally, if you journal every day, you will
record vital points to reflect upon, which can be
an added source of encouragement.

You can also reflect back on the magnificence
of previous days!

As we continue on this life's journey, there will be
some very difficult and dark days, as well as,
some very luminous days.

But we know that in the most trying times,
our faith will be challenged, as we grow.

These challenges serve to develop patience, and
patience adds to hope, and hope aids in creating
experience, and experience makes belief stronger
so that we are not ashamed.

The outcome then is, increased faith and new
experiences. This will
help in each individual's Faith Continuum!!

So Read, Reflect, and Write!!

Enjoy the Goodness of God in Your Life's
"Every Day Miracles"

Instructions for your daily entries

Read the Poem for that month
Read and Meditate on the scripture, then write your
reflections
On your good days rejoice, and on not so good days,
write your feelings, explain
your emotions, so that they can be handled in a positive,
healthy way.

Consider these questions:
What new covenant have you made, that you will work
on intentionally this year?
What are the things you are thankful for?
What things or people have you been afraid of?
What things have hindered you most?
Are there any things you began and have not
completed?
Are there areas that require clarification, prior to
completing?
How has daily journaling aided you in reevaluating,
and reorganizing your daily thinking, and actions?
What is your vision for yourself/family?
How can you be instrumental in getting your vision
accomplished?
In what areas would you like to develop more?
Write down your strengths and weaknesses. Be inten-
tional about working on both.

What gifts and talents do you have? Are you sharing
them with others?

What are your thoughts regarding righteousness and
wickedness?

Have your views changed as you reflect on the
scriptures?

How is journaling affecting your thoughts about yourself,
how you interact

with others, and your outlook for the future?

Review your reflections. Note your progress
and growth.

Do you see the Miracles?

January

New Beginnings

This is a new beginning,
Another year has come and gone,
I will sing aloud the praise of God,
In melody with my heart's song.

This is a new beginning,
the past is gone for sure,
So now a new day, a new year,
There is just so much more.

We may have thought we had enough,
But still we stand with both hands raised,
We made it through some days that were rough,
With our faithful God to be praised!

Today we say goodbye to old,
And welcome all that's new,
Move forward with high expectation,
And see what God has for you!

"In the beginning God created the heaven and the earth." Genesis 1:1

January
1

_____

_____

_____

_____

_____

_____

_____

_____

_____

_____

_____

_____

_____

_____

_____

_____

_____

_____

_____

"In the beginning was the Word, and the Word was with
God, and the Word was God." John 1:1

January
2

_____

_____

_____

_____

_____

_____

_____

_____

_____

_____

_____

_____

_____

_____

_____

_____

_____

_____

_____

_____

_____

"The fear of the Lord is the beginning
of wisdom:" Proverbs 1:7

January
3

"I am Alpha and Omega, the beginning and the ending, saith the Lord, which is, and which was, and which is to come, the Almighty." Revelation 1:8

January
4

_____

_____

_____

_____

_____

_____

_____

_____

_____

_____

_____

_____

_____

_____

_____

_____

_____

_____

_____

_____

"The fear of the Lord is the beginning of wisdom;
A good understanding have all those who do His
commandments, His praise endures forever." Psalm 111:10

January
5

Matthew 6:33 "But seek ye first the kingdom of God
and his righteousness, and all these things shall be
added unto you."

January
6

"This month shall be unto you the beginning of
months: it shall be the first month of the year to you"
Exodus 12:2

January
7

_____

_____

_____

_____

_____

_____

_____

_____

_____

_____

_____

_____

_____

_____

_____

_____

_____

_____

_____

"But when he saw the wind boisterous, he was afraid;
and beginning to sink, he cried, saying, Lord, save
me." Matthew 14:30

January
8

_____

_____

_____

_____

_____

_____

_____

_____

_____

_____

_____

_____

_____

_____

_____

_____

_____

_____

_____

_____

"A land which the Lord thy God careth for: the eyes
of the Lord thy God are always upon it, from the
beginning of the year even unto the end of the year."
Deuteronomy 11:12

January
9

_____

_____

_____

_____

_____

_____

_____

_____

_____

_____

_____

_____

_____

_____

_____

_____

_____

_____

_____

"And he answered and said unto them, Have ye not read, that he which made them at the beginning made them male and female." Matthew 19:4

January
10

"Reuben, thou art my firstborn; my might, and the
beginning of my strength, the excellency of dignity, and
the excellency of power." Genesis 49:3

January
11

"Also I will ordain a place for my people Israel, and will
plant them, and they shall dwell in their place, and shall
be moved no more; neither shall the children of wickedness
waste them any more, as at the beginning." I Chronicles 17:9

January
12

"He saith unto them, Moses because of the hardness of your hearts suffered you to put away your wives: but from the beginning it was not so." Matthew 19:8

January
13

_____

_____

_____

_____

_____

_____

_____

_____

_____

_____

_____

_____

_____

_____

_____

_____

_____

_____

_____

_____

"Though thy beginning was small, yet thy latter end
should greatly increase." Job 8:7

January
14

_____

_____

_____

_____

_____

_____

_____

_____

_____

_____

_____

_____

_____

_____

_____

_____

_____

_____

_____

_____

"Forasmuch as many have taken in hand to set forth in
Order a declaration of those things which are most surely
Believed among us, Even as they delivered them unto us,
which from the beginning were eyewitnesses, and ministers
of the word." Luke 1:1-2

January
15

_____

_____

_____

_____

_____

_____

_____

_____

_____

_____

_____

_____

_____

_____

_____

_____

_____

_____

_____

_____

"Thy word is true from the beginning: and every one of thy righteous judgements endureth for ever." Psalm 119:160

January
16

_____

_____

_____

_____

_____

_____

_____

_____

_____

_____

_____

_____

_____

_____

_____

_____

_____

_____

_____

_____

_____

"And beginning at Moses and all the prophets, he expounded
unto them in all the scriptures the things concerning himself,"
Luke 24:27

January
17

"The Lord possessed me in the beginning of his way, before his works of old." Proverbs 8:22

January
18

_____

_____

_____

_____

_____

_____

_____

_____

_____

_____

_____

_____

_____

_____

_____

_____

_____

_____

_____

_____

"This beginning of miracles did Jesus in Cana of Galilee, and manifested forth his glory; and his disciples believed on him." John 2:11

January
19

_____

_____

_____

_____

_____

_____

_____

_____

_____

_____

_____

_____

_____

_____

_____

_____

_____

_____

_____

"Then said they unto him, Who art thou? And Jesus saith unto them, Even the same that I said unto you from the beginning." John 8:25

January
20

_____

_____

_____

_____

_____

_____

_____

_____

_____

_____

_____

_____

_____

_____

_____

_____

_____

_____

_____

_____

_____

"The beginning of strife is as when one letteth out water: therefore leave off contention, before it be meddled with." Proverbs 17:14

January
21

_____

_____

_____

_____

_____

_____

_____

_____

_____

_____

_____

_____

_____

_____

_____

_____

_____

_____

_____

_____

"The same was in the beginning with God."
John 1:2

January
22

_____

_____

_____

_____

_____

_____

_____

_____

_____

_____

_____

_____

_____

_____

_____

_____

_____

_____

_____

"An inheritance may be gotten hastily at the
beginning; but the end thereof shall not be blessed."
Proverbs 20:21

January
23

"And ye also shall bear witness, because ye have been with me from the beginning." John 15:27

January
24

"Better is the end of a thing then the beginning
Thereof: and the patient in spirit is better than the
Proud in spirit." Ecclesiastes 7:8

January
25

_____

_____

_____

_____

_____

_____

_____

_____

_____

_____

_____

_____

_____

_____

_____

_____

_____

_____

_____

"Being confident of this very thing, that
he which hath begun a good work in you will perform
it until the day of Jesus Christ," Philippians 1:6

January
26

_____

_____

_____

_____

_____

_____

_____

_____

_____

_____

_____

_____

_____

_____

_____

_____

_____

_____

"Who hath wrought and done it, calling the generations
from the beginning? I the Lord, the first, and with the last;
I am he." Isaiah 41:4

January
27

_____

_____

_____

_____

_____

_____

_____

_____

_____

_____

_____

_____

_____

_____

_____

_____

_____

_____

_____

"And as I began to speak, the Holy Ghost fell
on them, as on us at the beginning." Acts 11:15

January
28

"He hath made every thing beautiful in his time: also
he hath set the world in their heart, so that no man can
find out the work that God maketh from the beginning to
the end." Ecclesiastes 3:11

January
29

_____

_____

_____

_____

_____

_____

_____

_____

_____

_____

_____

_____

_____

_____

_____

_____

_____

_____

_____

"Known unto God are all his works from the beginning of the world." Acts 15:18

January
30

"For, behold, I create new heavens and a new earth: and the former shall not be remembered, nor come into mind." Isaiah 65:17

January
31

_____

_____

_____

_____

_____

_____

_____

_____

_____

_____

_____

_____

_____

_____

_____

_____

_____

_____

February

Pursue your Passion

Pursue your passion, run after your dream,
It's not as far off as it may seem!
Passion pushes you to do, the very thing you like to,
Passion wakes you, and makes you move,
Won't let you walk in another's shoes.

Pulling, stretching, uncomfortable at times,
Persistent thoughts never leave your mind.
But rest you can't, it's time to grow,
So much is waiting, you've got to go.

Pursue that passion or sleep you won't
Tossing with questions, what if I don't,
What if you fail, but what if you win,
The whole world will lose what you've got to give.

To keep that treasure that throbs your heart,
You are the key to another's start,
Moving toward promise that's meant to be,
Or that Passion wouldn't fight so, Don't you see.

So pursue your passion, run after your dream,
It's not as far off as it may seem.
Pursue your passion, press to receive,
All things are possible, but you must believe!

Pursue your passion, it will make you free,
Breaking bonds of limitation,
Forward to your destiny!

"He that dwelleth in the secret place of the
most High shall abide under the shadow of
the Almighty." Psalm 91:1

February
1

_____

_____

_____

_____

_____

_____

_____

_____

_____

_____

_____

_____

_____

_____

_____

_____

_____

"Endeavoring to keep the unity of the Spirit
in the bond of peace." Ephesians 4:3

February
2

_____

_____

_____

_____

_____

_____

_____

_____

_____

_____

_____

_____

_____

_____

_____

_____

_____

_____

_____

_____

_____

_____

"I will say of the Lord, He is my refuge and my
fortress; my God in him will I trust." Psalm 91: 2

February
3

_____

_____

_____

_____

_____

_____

_____

_____

_____

_____

_____

_____

_____

_____

_____

_____

_____

_____

_____

_____

_____

"One God and Father of all, who is above all,
and through all, and in you all." Ephesians 4:6

February
4

"Surely he shall deliver thee from the snare of the
fowler, and from the noisome pestilence." Psalm 91:3

February
5

_____

_____

_____

_____

_____

_____

_____

_____

_____

_____

_____

_____

_____

_____

_____

_____

_____

_____

_____

"But unto every one of us is given grace according
to the measure of the gift of Christ." Ephesians 4:7

February
6

"He shall cover thee with his feathers, and under
his wings shalt thou trust: his truth shall be thy
shield and buckler." Psalm 91:4

February
7

_____

_____

_____

_____

_____

_____

_____

_____

_____

_____

_____

_____

_____

_____

_____

_____

_____

_____

_____

"Nay, in all these things we are more than conquerors
through him that loved us." Romans8:37

February
8

"Thou shalt not be afraid for the terror by night,
nor for the arrow that flieth by day;" Psalm 91:5

February
9

_____

_____

_____

_____

_____

_____

_____

_____

_____

_____

_____

_____

_____

_____

_____

_____

_____

_____

_____

_____

"What shall we then say to these things? If God
be for us, who can be against us?" Romans 8:31

February
10

_____

_____

_____

_____

_____

_____

_____

_____

_____

_____

_____

_____

_____

_____

_____

_____

_____

_____

_____

_____

_____

"A thousand shall fall at thy side, and ten thousand
at thy right hand; but it shall not come nigh thee."
Psalm 91:7

February
11

"Therefore if any man be in Christ, he a new creature: old things are passed away: behold, all things are become new." 2 Corinthians 5:17

February
12

_____

_____

_____

_____

_____

_____

_____

_____

_____

_____

_____

_____

_____

_____

_____

_____

_____

_____

"Only with thine eyes shalt thou behold and
see the reward of the wicked." Psalm 91:8

February
13

"But God commendeth his love toward us, in that while we were yet sinners, Christ died for us." Romans 5:8

February 14

_____
_____
_____
_____
_____
_____
_____
_____
_____
_____
_____
_____
_____
_____
_____
_____
_____
_____
_____
_____
_____
_____

"Because thou hast made the Lord, which is my refuge,
even the most High, thy habitation;" Psalm 91:9

February
15

_____

_____

_____

_____

_____

_____

_____

_____

_____

_____

_____

_____

_____

_____

_____

_____

_____

_____

_____

_____

"I am crucified with Christ: nevertheless I live;
yet not I, but Christ liveth in me: and the life which I
now live in the flesh I live by the faith of the Son of
God, who loved me, and gave himself for me,"
Galatians 2:20

February
16

"There shall no evil befall thee, neither shall any plague come nigh thy dwelling." Psalm 91:10

February
17

_____

_____

_____

_____

_____

_____

_____

_____

_____

_____

_____

_____

_____

_____

_____

_____

_____

_____

_____

_____

_____

"If we confess our sins, he is faithful and
just to forgive us our sins, and to cleanse us from all
unrighteousness." 1 John 1:9_

February
18

"For he shall give his angels charge over thee,
to keep thee in all thy ways." Psalm 91:11

February
19

_____

_____

_____

_____

_____

_____

_____

_____

_____

_____

_____

_____

_____

_____

_____

_____

_____

_____

_____

_____

_____

"With all lowliness and meekness, with
longsuffering, forbearing one another in love;
Ephesians 4:2 "

February
20

_____
_____
_____
_____
_____
_____
_____
_____
_____
_____
_____
_____
_____
_____
_____
_____
_____
_____
_____

"They shall bear thee up in their hands, lest
thou dash thy foot against a stone." Psalm 91:12

February
21

"He that descended is the same also that
 ascended up far above all heavens, that he might fill all
 things." Ephesians 4:10

February
22

_____

_____

_____

_____

_____

_____

_____

_____

_____

_____

_____

_____

_____

_____

_____

_____

_____

_____

_____

_____

"Thou shalt tread upon the lion and adder:
the young lion and the dragon shalt thou trample under
feet." Psalm 91:13

February
23

_____

_____

_____

_____

_____

_____

_____

_____

_____

_____

_____

_____

_____

_____

_____

_____

_____

_____

"Even so the tongue is a little member and
boasteth great things. Behold, how great a matter a
little fire kindleth!" James 3:5

February
24

_____

_____

_____

_____

_____

_____

_____

_____

_____

_____

_____

_____

_____

_____

_____

_____

_____

_____

_____

_____

"Because he hath set his love upon me,
therefore will I deliver him: I will set him on high,
because he hath known my name." Psalm 91:14

February
25

"For with the heart man believeth unto
righteousness: and with the mouth confession is made
unto salvation." Romans 10:10

February
26

_____

_____

_____

_____

_____

_____

_____

_____

_____

_____

_____

_____

_____

_____

_____

_____

_____

_____

"He shall call upon me, and I will answer him: I will
be with him in trouble; I will deliver him, and honour
him." Psalm 91:15

February
27

"I exhort therefore, that, first of all, supplications, prayers, intercessions, and giving of thanks, be made for all men;" 1 Timothy 2:1

February
28

_____

_____

_____

_____

_____

_____

_____

_____

_____

_____

_____

_____

_____

_____

_____

_____

_____

_____

_____

"With long life will I satisfy him, and shew him
my salvation." Psalm 91:16

February
29

_____

_____

_____

_____

_____

_____

_____

_____

_____

_____

_____

_____

_____

_____

_____

_____

_____

_____

_____

_____

March

Dreams

Dreams are conversations, pictures in your sleep,
So many precious things you want to keep,
They can also be whispers from God to us,
The thoughts from his heart that we can trust.
To tell us secrets unspoken by day,
To encourage, strengthen, and comfort us on our way.

Through this life's journey which can be hard,
Only the Lord can say which way we must trod,
We must lean and depend, listen and see,
To be shown the course that is to be.

So continue to dream, meditate and pursue,
All our dear Father has planned for you
Then live, love and share what you receive,
So that others around you will
Dream and Believe!!

"But ye shall receive power, after that the Holy Ghost
is come upon you: and ye shall be witnesses unto me
both in Jerusalem, and all Judaea, and in Samaria, and unto
the uttermost part of the earth." Acts 1:8

March
1

For I am the LORD thy God, the Holy One of Israel, thy Saviour: I gave Egypt for thy ransom, Ethiopia and Seba for thee." Isaiah 43:3

March
2

"Casting all your care upon him;
for he careth for you." I Peter 5:7

March
3

_____

_____

_____

_____

_____

_____

_____

_____

_____

_____

_____

_____

_____

_____

_____

_____

_____

_____

_____

_____

_____

_____

_____

"But the Lord said unto me, Say not, I am a child:
for thou shalt go to all that I shall send thee, and
whatsoever I command thee thou shalt speak.
Jeremiah 1:7

March
4

"No man also seweth a piece of new cloth on an old garment: else the new piece that filled it up taketh away from the old, and the rent is made worse."
Mark 2:21

March
5

_____

_____

_____

_____

_____

_____

_____

_____

_____

_____

_____

_____

_____

_____

_____

_____

_____

_____

_____

_____

"I am the LORD thy God, which brought thee out of the land of Egypt, from the house of bondage. "
Exodus 20:2

March
6

"Jesus answered and said unto him, Verily, verily
I say unto thee, Except a man be born again, he
cannot see the kingdom of God." John 3:3

March
7

_____

_____

_____

_____

_____

_____

_____

_____

_____

_____

_____

_____

_____

_____

_____

_____

_____

_____

_____

_____

"And they went every one straight forward: whither the spirit was to go, they went; and they turned not when they went." Eziekiel 1:12

March
8

"Let your light so shine before men, that they may
see your good works, and glorify your Father which
is in heaven." Matthew 5:16

March
9

_____

_____

_____

_____

_____

_____

_____

_____

_____

_____

_____

_____

_____

_____

_____

_____

_____

_____

_____

_____

_____

"A man's heart deviseth his way: but the Lord
directeth his steps." Proverbs 16:9

March
10

"Mercy unto you, and peace, and love, be multiplied." Jude 1:2

March
11

_____

_____

_____

_____

_____

_____

_____

_____

_____

_____

_____

_____

_____

_____

_____

_____

_____

_____

_____

"Then was the secret revealed unto Daniel in a night vision. Then Daniel blessed the God of heaven."
Daniel 2:1

March
12

_____

_____

_____

_____

_____

_____

_____

_____

_____

_____

_____

_____

_____

_____

_____

_____

_____

_____

_____

"And Jesus answering saith unto them,
have faith in God." Mark 11:22

March
13

_____

_____

_____

_____

_____

_____

_____

_____

_____

_____

_____

_____

_____

_____

_____

_____

_____

_____

_____

_____

_____

_____

"Then will I go unto the altar of God, unto
God my exceeding joy: yea, upon the harp will I praise
thee, O God my God." Psalm 43:4

March
14

"His mother saith unto the servants, Whatsoever he saith unto you, do it." John 2:5

March
15

_____

_____

_____

_____

_____

_____

_____

_____

_____

_____

_____

_____

_____

_____

_____

_____

_____

_____

_____

_____

"Save me, O God, by thy name, and judge
me by thy strength." Psalm 54:1

March
16

"For it is written, He shall give his angels charge over thee, to keep thee:" Luke 4:10

March
17

The Lord is my light and my salvation; whom
shall I fear? The Lord is strength of my life; of whom shall
I be afraid?" Luke 4:10

March
18

_____

_____

_____

_____

_____

_____

_____

_____

_____

_____

_____

_____

_____

_____

_____

_____

_____

_____

"By which also ye are saved, if ye keep in memory
what I preached unto you, unless ye have believed
in vain." 1 Corinthians 15:2

March
19

_____

_____

_____

_____

_____

_____

_____

_____

_____

_____

_____

_____

_____

_____

_____

_____

_____

_____

_____

"And the Lord have removed men far away, and there
be a great forsaking in the midst of the land." Isaiah 6:12

March
20

_____

_____

_____

_____

_____

_____

_____

_____

_____

_____

_____

_____

_____

_____

_____

_____

_____

_____

_____

_____

_____

_____

_____

"I do not frustrate the grace of God: for if righteousness come by the law, then Christ is dead in vain." Galatians 2:21

March
21

_____

_____

_____

_____

_____

_____

_____

_____

_____

_____

_____

_____

_____

_____

_____

_____

_____

_____

_____

_____

"Wherefore will ye plead with me? ye all have transgressed against me, saith the LORD. "
Jeremiah 2:29

March
22

"And this commandment have we from him, That
he who loveth God love his brother also." 1 John 4:21

March
23

_____

_____

_____

_____

_____

_____

_____

_____

_____

_____

_____

_____

_____

_____

_____

_____

_____

_____

_____

_____

"Wash me thoroughly from mine iniquity, and cleanse
me from my sin" Psalm 51:2

March
24

"For this is the love of God, that we keep his commandments: and his commandments are not grievous." 1 John 5:3

March
25

_____

_____

_____

_____

_____

_____

_____

_____

_____

_____

_____

_____

_____

_____

_____

_____

_____

_____

_____

_____

_____

"To give subtility to the simple, to the young man knowledge and discretion." Proverbs 1:4

March
26

"Jesus said unto him, Thou shalt love the Lord thy
God with all thy heart, and with all thy soul, and with
all thy mind." Matthew 22:37

March
27

"A wise man will hear, and will increase learning; and
a man of understanding shall attain unto wise counsels:"
Proverbs 1:5

March
28

"Beloved, I wish above all things that thou mayest prosper
and be in health, even as thy soul prospereth." 3 John 1:2

March
29

"To understand a proverb, and the interpretation; the words of the wise, and their dark sayings." Proverbs 1:6

March
30

_____

_____

_____

_____

_____

_____

_____

_____

_____

_____

_____

_____

_____

_____

_____

_____

_____

_____

_____

_____

"Therefore I say unto you, Take no thought for your life, what ye shall eat, or what ye shall drink; nor yet for your body, what ye shall put on. Is not life more than meat, and the body than raiment?
Matthew 6:25

March
31

April

Rain/Reign

When the sun goes into hiding,
All of nature moves in sync,
Clouds come out awaiting perfect pearls,
Forming that much-needed drink.

As we turn toward the heavens,
Without a word, the rain has, come,
To soothe that which is parched,
On the earth, sprouts of life anew begun.

Receiving God's precious spring
To wash and to refresh,
Making everything smell clean,
And the lilies helps to dress.

As we view the rain outside,
How it provides for all we see,
The word will wash sin-stained hearts and minds,
Giving peace and truth to make us free.

Like the rain pours on our natural flesh
Let the Spirit reign inside,
We only must submit, to Him,
To come in and abide.

"Beloved, thou doest faithfully whatsoever thou
doest to the brethren, and to strangers;" 3 John 1:5

April
1

_____

_____

_____

_____

_____

_____

_____

_____

_____

_____

_____

_____

_____

_____

_____

_____

_____

_____

_____

_____

"The tongue of the wise useth knowledge aright: but
the mouth of fools poureth out foolishness." Proverbs 15:2

April
2

"If the Son therefore shall make you free, ye shall be free indeed." St. John 8:36

April
3

_____

_____

_____

_____

_____

_____

_____

_____

_____

_____

_____

_____

_____

_____

_____

_____

_____

_____

"My son, hear the instruction of thy father, and
forsake not the law of thy mother:" Proverbs 1:8

April
4

_____

_____

_____

_____

_____

_____

_____

_____

_____

_____

_____

_____

_____

_____

_____

_____

_____

_____

_____

_____

_____

My brethren, be not many masters, knowing that we
Shall receive the greater condemnation." James 3:1

April
5

_____

_____

_____

_____

_____

_____

_____

_____

_____

_____

_____

_____

_____

_____

_____

_____

_____

_____

"And he laid it upon my mouth, and said, Lo, this
hath touched thy lips; and thine iniquity is taken away
and thy sin purged." Isaiah 6:7

April
6

"And saying, Repent ye: For the kingdom
of heaven is at hand." Matthew 3:2

April
7

"In the house of the righteous is much treasure:
but in revenues of the wicked is trouble."
Proverbs 15:6

April
8

"And thou, Lord in the beginning hast laid the foundation of the earth; and the heavens are the works of thine hands." Hebrews 1:10

April
9

"I charge you, O daughters of Jerusalem, that ye
stir not up, nor awake my love, until he please."
Song of Solomon 8:4

April
10

"For we are made partakers of Christ, if we hold the
beginning of our confidence steadfast unto the end."
Hebrews 3:14

April
11

_____

_____

_____

_____

_____

_____

_____

_____

_____

_____

_____

_____

_____

_____

_____

_____

_____

_____

_____

_____

"My people are destroyed for the lack of knowledge:
because thou hast rejected knowledge, I will also reject
thee, that thou shalt be no priest to me: seeing thou hast
forgotten the law of thy God, I will also forget thy children."
Hosea 4:6

April
12

"And saying, Where is the promise of his coming? For since the fathers fell asleep, all things continue as they were from the beginning of creation." 2 Peter 3:4

April
13

"Speak not in the ears of a fool: for he will despise
the wisdom of thy words." Proverbs 23:9

April
14

"He that committed sin is of the devil; for the devil sinneth from the beginning for this purpose the Son of God was manifested that he might destroy the works of the devil." 1 John 3:8

April
15

"Blow ye the trumpet in Zion, and sound an alarm in my holy mountain: let all the inhabitants of the land tremble: for the day of the Lord cometh, for it is nigh at hand;" Joel 2:1

April
16

"For this is the message that ye heard from the beginning, that we should love one another." 1 John 3:11

April 17

_____
_____
_____
_____
_____
_____
_____
_____
_____
_____
_____
_____
_____
_____
_____
_____
_____
_____
_____
_____
_____

"Blessed are the undefiled in the way, who walk
in the law of the Lord." Psalm 119:1

April
18

"Therefore, if any man be in Christ, he is a new creature: old things are passed away; behold. all things are become new."
2 Corinthians 5:17

April
19

_____

_____

_____

_____

_____

_____

_____

_____

_____

_____

_____

_____

_____

_____

_____

_____

_____

_____

_____

_____

"The law of truth was in his mouth, and iniquity was not found in his lips: he walked with me in peace and equity, and did turn many away from iniquity."
Malachi 2:6

April
20

_____

_____

_____

_____

_____

_____

_____

_____

_____

_____

_____

_____

_____

_____

_____

_____

_____

_____

_____

_____

"There is no fear in love; but perfect love casteth out fear; because fear hath torment. He that feareth is not made perfect in love." 1 John 4:18

April
21

"And the priests could not enter into the house of the Lord, because the glory of the Lord had filled the Lord's house." 2 Chronicles 7:2

April
22

_____

_____

_____

_____

_____

_____

_____

_____

_____

_____

_____

_____

_____

_____

_____

_____

_____

_____

_____

_____

"That ye put off concerning the former conversation the old man, which is corrupt according to the deceitful lusts;" Ephesians 4:22

April
23

_____

_____

_____

_____

_____

_____

_____

_____

_____

_____

_____

_____

_____

_____

_____

_____

_____

_____

_____

_____

_____

"But of the fruit of the tree which is in the midst of the garden, God hath said, Ye shall not eat of it, neither shall ye touch it, lest ye die." Genesis 3:3

April
24

"And seeing the multitudes, he went up into a mountain:
and when he was set, his disciples came unto him:"
Matthew 5:1

April
25

_____

_____

_____

_____

_____

_____

_____

_____

_____

_____

_____

_____

_____

_____

_____

_____

_____

_____

"O lord God of my salvation, I have cried day and night
before thee:" Psalm 88:1

April
26

"I do not frustrate the grace of God: for if righteousness
come by the law, then Christ is dead in vain." Galatians 2:21

April
27

_____

_____

_____

_____

_____

_____

_____

_____

_____

_____

_____

_____

_____

_____

_____

_____

_____

_____

_____

_____

_____

_____

"A good name is rather to be chosen than great riches,
 and loving favor rather than silver and gold." Proverbs 22:1

April
28

_____

_____

_____

_____

_____

_____

_____

_____

_____

_____

_____

_____

_____

_____

_____

_____

_____

_____

_____

_____

_____

"And he took them up in his arms, put his hands
upon them, and blessed them." Mark 10:16

April
29

_____

_____

_____

_____

_____

_____

_____

_____

_____

_____

_____

_____

_____

_____

_____

_____

_____

_____

_____

"The Lord is my shepherd; I shall not want."
Psalm 23:1

April
30

May

The Wonder of A Woman

She rises with strength and courage each day,
Focused on others, graciously willing to pray,
Her thoughts on those around her,
and meeting their needs,
She plants and she waters,
trusting the Lord with the seeds.

Planted in every place her feet land,
It's God's grace and mercy that cause her to stand,
The wonder of this woman who is clothed from above,
God, the source her strength and undying love.
It's Jesus the Christ who she sought, and has found,
For no other place can such power abound.

This special woman by all is called blessed,
She's weathered great storms, passed life's many tests,
She is mother, she's wife, but dear friend to all,
The wonder woman of God who will answer His call.

"As it is written, There is none righteous, no,
not one:" Romans 3:10

May
1

_____

_____

_____

_____

_____

_____

_____

_____

_____

_____

_____

_____

_____

_____

_____

_____

_____

_____

_____

_____

"I will bless the Lord at all times: His praise
shall continually be in my mouth." Psalm 34:1

May
2

"Honour thy father and mother; which
is the first commandment with promise;"
Ephesians 6:2

May
3

"But I would no hearken unto Balaam; therefore
he blessed you still: so I delivered you out of his
hand." Joshua 24:10

May
4

_____

_____

_____

_____

_____

_____

_____

_____

_____

_____

_____

_____

_____

_____

_____

_____

_____

_____

"That which is born of the flesh is flesh; and
that which is born of the Spirit is spirit." John 3:6

May
5

_____

_____

_____

_____

_____

_____

_____

_____

_____

_____

_____

_____

_____

_____

_____

_____

_____

_____

_____

_____

_____

"Every place that the sole of your foot shall tread upon , that have I given unto you, as I said unto Moses." Joshua 1:3

May
6

_____

_____

_____

_____

_____

_____

_____

_____

_____

_____

_____

_____

_____

_____

_____

_____

_____

_____

_____

"I can do all things through Christ
which strengtheneth me." Philippians 4:13

May
7

_____

_____

_____

_____

_____

_____

_____

_____

_____

_____

_____

_____

_____

_____

_____

_____

_____

_____

_____

_____

_____

_____

"Who hath believed our report? And to whom is the arm of the Lord revealed?"
Isaiah 53:1

May
8

_____

_____

_____

_____

_____

_____

_____

_____

_____

_____

_____

_____

_____

_____

_____

_____

_____

_____

_____

"Out of same mouth proceedeth blessing and
cursing. My brethren, these things ought not so
to be." James 3:10

May
9

"And it came to pass, when the congregation
was gathered against Moses and against Aaron,
that they looked toward the tabernacle of the
congregation: and, behold, the cloud covered it,
and the glory of the Lord appeared." Numbers16:42

May
10

"They are all gone out of the way, they are together become unprofitable; there is none that doeth good, no, not one." Romans 3:12

May
11

"O Lord God of my salvation, I have cried day
and night before thee: Let my prayer come before
thee: incline thine ear unto my cry;" Psalm 88: 1-2

May
12

"And now abide faith, hope, love, these three; but the greatest of these is love."
1 Corinthians 13:13

May
13

"Yea, he loved the people; all his saints
are in thy hand: and they sat down at thy
feet; every one shall receive of thy words."
Deuteronomy 33:3

May
14

_____

_____

_____

_____

_____

_____

_____

_____

_____

_____

_____

_____

_____

_____

_____

_____

_____

_____

_____

"Let not your heart be troubled: ye believe
in God, believe also in me." John 14:1

May
15

_____

_____

_____

_____

_____

_____

_____

_____

_____

_____

_____

_____

_____

_____

_____

_____

_____

_____

_____

"Arise; for this matter belongeth unto thee: we also
will be with thee: be of good courage, and do it."
Ezra 10:4

May
16

_____

_____

_____

_____

_____

_____

_____

_____

_____

_____

_____

_____

_____

_____

_____

_____

"For John truly baptized with water; but ye shall be baptized with the Holy Ghost not many days hence." Acts 1:5

May
17

_____

_____

_____

_____

_____

_____

_____

_____

_____

_____

_____

_____

_____

_____

_____

_____

_____

_____

And they went every one straight forward:
whither the spirit was to go, they went; and they turned
not when they went." Ezekiel 1:12

May
18

_____

_____

_____

_____

_____

_____

_____

_____

_____

_____

_____

_____

_____

_____

_____

_____

_____

_____

_____

"Even the righteousness of God which is by
faith of Jesus Christ unto all and upon all them
that believe: for there is no difference:"
Romans 3:22

May
19

_____

_____

_____

_____

_____

_____

_____

_____

_____

_____

_____

_____

_____

_____

_____

_____

_____

_____

"And he said, I heard thy voice in the
garden, and I was afraid, because I was naked; and
I hid myself." Genesis 3:10

May
20

_____

_____

_____

_____

_____

_____

_____

_____

_____

_____

_____

_____

_____

_____

_____

_____

_____

_____

"Not given to wine, no striker, not greedy of filthy lucre; but patient, not a brawler, not covetous;"
1 Timothy 3:3

May
21

_____

_____

_____

_____

_____

_____

_____

_____

_____

_____

_____

_____

_____

_____

_____

_____

_____

_____

"Wherefore I will yet plead with you, saith the Lord,
and with your children's children will I plead."
Jeremiah 2:9

May
22

"Blessed are the poor in spirit: for
theirs is the kingdom of heaven." Matthew 5:3

May
23

"He revealeth the deep and secret things:
he knoweth what is in the darkness, and the light
dwelleth with him," Daniel 2:22

May
24

_____

_____

_____

_____

_____

_____

_____

_____

_____

_____

_____

_____

_____

_____

_____

_____

_____

_____

"But when he saw Jesus afar of, he ran and
 Worshipped him," Mark 5:6

May
25

"Trust in the Lord with all thine heart;
and lean not unto thine own understanding."
Proverbs 3:5

May
26

_____

_____

_____

_____

_____

_____

_____

_____

_____

_____

_____

_____

_____

_____

_____

_____

_____

_____

_____

_____

"Children, obey your parents in the
Lord: for this is right." Ephesians 6:1

May
27

_____

_____

_____

_____

_____

_____

_____

_____

_____

_____

_____

_____

_____

_____

_____

_____

_____

_____

_____

_____

_____

_____

_____

"In all thy ways acknowledge him, and he shall direct thy paths." Proverbs 3:6

May
28

"Hearken, my beloved brethren, Hath not God
chosen the poor of this world rich in faith, and
heirs of the kingdom which he hath promised
to them that love him?" James 2:5

May
29

"For the LORD giveth wisdom: out of his mouth
cometh knowledge and understanding."
Proverbs 2:6

May
30

_____

_____

_____

_____

_____

_____

_____

_____

_____

_____

_____

_____

_____

_____

_____

_____

_____

_____

"So that we may boldly say, The Lord is my helper,
and I will not fear what man shall do unto me."
Hebrews 13:6

May
31

June

June

The Love of the Father
Our Father which art in Heaven we pray,
Do we really understand the love as we say?
The ways that are taught by Our Father above,
Are the ones we display as children of love.

We hallow Our Father with praise from our lips,
More in actions and living is shown,
To others who sense the warmth of a touch,
Brought with a price, now not our own.

Extending our hands, unselfish and kind,
With no conditions at all says He,
No matter what situation someone is in,
Our eyes a soul clearly sees.

A love so intense every blemish it hides
That which is left is His brightness and light,
We must remember in all that we do,
We must always love others
As your Father in Heaven loves You!

"Turn us again, O God, cause thy face to shine;
and we shall be saved." Psalm 80:3

June
1

"Behold my servant, whom I have chosen; my beloved, in whom my soul is well pleased: I will put my spirit upon him, and he shall shew judgement to the Gentiles." Matthew 12:18

June
2

"Speak unto the children of Israel, and say unto them,
I am the Lord your God. Leviticus 18:2

June
3

_____

_____

_____

_____

_____

_____

_____

_____

_____

_____

_____

_____

_____

_____

_____

_____

_____

_____

_____

_____

_____

"If ye endure chastening, God dealeth with you as with sons;
for what son is he whom the father chasteneth not?"
Hebrews 12:7

June
4

"A fool uttereth all his mind: but a wise man keepeth it in till afterwards." Proverbs 29:11

June
5

"Which hope we have as an anchor of the soul, both sure and stedfast, and which entereth into that within the veil," Hebrews 6:19

June
6

"Fear thou not; for I am with thee: be not dismayed; for I am
thy God: I will strengthen thee; yea, I will help thee; yea, I will
uphold thee with the right hand of my righteousness." Isaiah 41:10

June
7

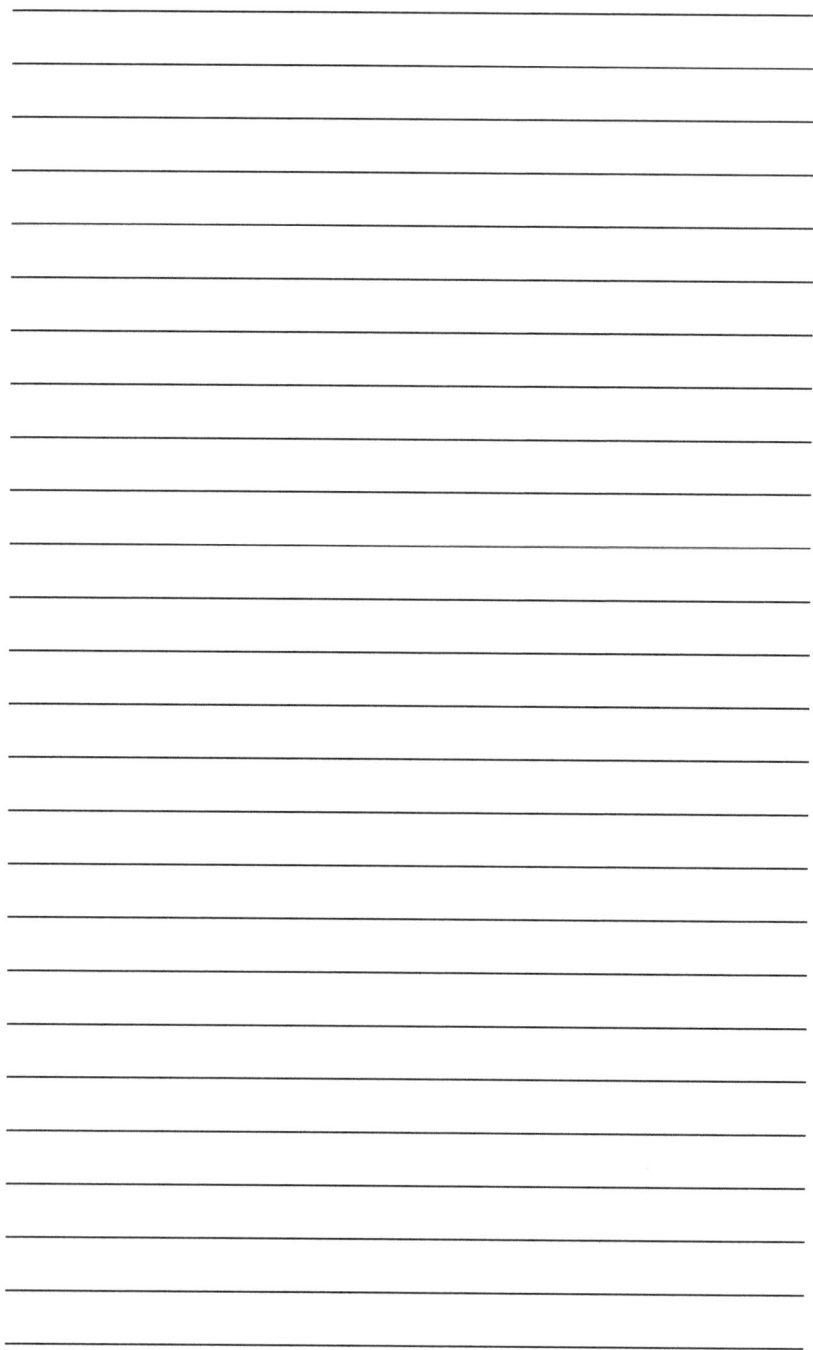

"And when he had called unto him his twelve disciples, he gave them
power against unclean spirits, to cast them out, and to heal all manner
of sickness and all manner of disease." Matthew 10:1

June
8

"Wine is a mocker, strong drink is raging: and whosoever is deceived thereby is not wise." Proverbs 20:1

June
9

_____

_____

_____

_____

_____

_____

_____

_____

_____

_____

_____

_____

_____

_____

_____

_____

_____

_____

"Heal the sick, cleanse the lepers, raise the dead, cast out devils: freely ye have received, freely give." Matthew 10:8

June
10

"Teach me, O Lord, the way of thy statutes; and I shall keep it unto the end." Psalm 119:33

June
11

_____
_____
_____
_____
_____
_____
_____
_____
_____
_____
_____
_____
_____
_____
_____
_____
_____
_____
_____
_____
_____

"And whosoever shall not receive you, nor hear your words, when ye depart out of that house or city, shake off the dust of your feet."
Matthew 10:14

June
12

_____

_____

_____

_____

_____

_____

_____

_____

_____

_____

_____

_____

_____

_____

_____

_____

_____

_____

_____

"Give me understanding, and I shall keep thy law; yea, I shall observe with my whole heart." Psalm 119:34

June
13

"And when one of them that sat at meat with him heard these things, he said unto him, Blessed is he that shall eat bread in the kingdom of God."
Luke 14:15

June
14

_____

_____

_____

_____

_____

_____

_____

_____

_____

_____

_____

_____

_____

_____

_____

_____

_____

_____

_____

"Make me to go in the path of thy commandments; for therein do I delight." Psalm 119:35

June
15

_____

_____

_____

_____

_____

_____

_____

_____

_____

_____

_____

_____

_____

_____

_____

_____

_____

_____

"And as he journeyed, he came near Damascus: and suddenly there
shined round about him a light from heaven:" Acts 9:3

June
16

"Incline my heart unto thy testimonies, and not to covetousness."
Psalm 119:36

June
17

_____

_____

_____

_____

_____

_____

_____

_____

_____

_____

_____

_____

_____

_____

_____

_____

_____

_____

_____

_____

_____

_____

"And he fell to the earth, and heard a voice saying unto him, Saul, Saul, why persecutes thou me?" Acts 9:4

June
18

"Turn away mine eyes from beholding vanity; and quicken thou me in thy way." Psalm 119:37

June
19

_____
_____
_____
_____
_____
_____
_____
_____
_____
_____
_____
_____
_____
_____
_____
_____
_____
_____
_____
_____
_____
_____

"And he said, Who art thou, Lord? And the Lord said, I am Jesus
whom thou persecutes it is hard for thee to kick against the pricks."
Acts 9:5

June
20

"Stablish thy word unto thy servant, who is devoted to thy fear."
Psalm 119:38

June
21

"And he trembling and astonished said, Lord, what wilt thou have me to do? And the Lord said unto him, Arise, and go into the city, and it shall be told thee what thou must do." Acts 9:6

June
22

_____

_____

_____

_____

_____

_____

_____

_____

_____

_____

_____

_____

_____

_____

_____

_____

_____

_____

"Turn away my reproach which I fear: for thy judgments are good."
Psalm 119:39

June
23

_____

_____

_____

_____

_____

_____

_____

_____

_____

_____

_____

_____

_____

_____

_____

_____

_____

_____

_____

_____

_____

_____

_____

"And these things write we unto you, that your joy may be full."
1 John 1:4

June
24

"Thou shalt be visited of the Lord of hosts with thunder, and with earthquake, and great noise, with storm and tempest, and the flame of devouring fire." Isaiah 29:6

June 25

"Let your conversation be without covetousness; and be content with such things as ye have: for he hath said, I will never leave thee, nor forsake thee." Hebrews 13:5

June
26

_____

_____

_____

_____

_____

_____

_____

_____

_____

_____

_____

_____

_____

_____

_____

_____

_____

_____

_____

"For I will restore health unto thee, and I will heal thee of thy wounds, saith the LORD; because they called thee an Outcast, saying, This is Zion, whom no man seeketh after." Jeremiah 30:17

June
27

"Jesus Christ the same yesterday, and today, and for ever." Hebrews 13:8

June
28

_____
_____
_____
_____
_____
_____
_____
_____
_____
_____
_____
_____
_____
_____
_____
_____
_____
_____
_____
_____
_____
_____

"The spoilers are come upon all high places through the wilderness: for the sword of the LORD shall devour from the one end of the land even to the other end of the land: no flesh shall have peace." Jeremiah 12:12

June
29

"But thanks be to God, which giveth us the victory through our
Lord Jesus Christ." 1 Corinthians 15:57

June
30

July

Surrounded by God

I took myself out for a ride,
Just to see what I could see,
And the more I rode, the more I saw,
Of God's awesome scenery.

The sky was clear, a soft shade of blue,
Small clouds were like marshmellows passing through,
The colorful trees were a delight to see,
Like a pastel pallet laid out before me.

I stopped and got out, and there was a stream,
Just like the one you might see in a dream,
The water was cold, but as clear as could be,
And then I thought, just another one of God's
mysteries.

I lingered there a while, where I released all my cares,
And felt the warming comfort,
for I knew my God was there,
Just being in his presence is the greatest joy I know,
And His promise to be with me, no matter where I go.

"Behold, the days come, saith the Lord, that I will make a
new covenant with the house of Israel, and with the house
of Judah:" Jeremiah 31:31

July
1

"(For we walk by faith, not by sight:)" 2 Corinthians 5:7

July
2

_____

_____

_____

_____

_____

_____

_____

_____

_____

_____

_____

_____

_____

_____

_____

_____

_____

_____

_____

_____

"The proverbs of Solomon. A wise son maketh a glad father:
but a foolish son *is* the heaviness of his mother." Proverbs 10:1

July
3

"That by two immutable things, in which it was impossible for God to lie, we might have a strong consolation, who have fled for refuge to lay hold upon the hope set before us." Hebrews 6:18

July
4

"The LORD by wisdom hath founded the earth; by understanding hath he established the heavens." Proverbs 3:19

July
5

"That Christ may dwell in your hearts by faith; that ye, being rooted and grounded in love," Ephesians 3:17

July
6

"Unto me, who am less than the least of all saints, is this grace given, that I should preach among the Gentiles the unsearchable riches of Christ;" Ephesians 3:8

July
7

_____

_____

_____

_____

_____

_____

_____

_____

_____

_____

_____

_____

_____

_____

_____

_____

_____

_____

"Deliver thyself as a roe from the hand *of the hunter*, and as a bird
from the hand of the fowler." Proverbs 6:5

July
8

"Submit yourselves therefore to God. Resist the devil, and he will flee from you." James 4:7

July
9

_____

_____

_____

_____

_____

_____

_____

_____

_____

_____

_____

_____

_____

_____

_____

_____

_____

_____

_____

_____

"Thus speaketh the LORD of hosts, saying, This people say,
The time is not come, the time that the LORD'S house should
be built." Haggai 1:2

July
10

"Humble yourselves in the sight of the Lord, and he shall lift you up"
James 4:10

July
11

_____

_____

_____

_____

_____

_____

_____

_____

_____

_____

_____

_____

_____

_____

_____

_____

_____

_____

_____

_____

_____

"Now therefore thus saith the LORD of hosts; Consider your ways."
Haggai 1:5

July
12

"Be ye also patient; stablish your hearts: for the coming of the Lord draweth nigh." James 5:8

July
13

_____

_____

_____

_____

_____

_____

_____

_____

_____

_____

_____

_____

_____

_____

_____

_____

_____

_____

_____

_____

_____

"Beat your plowshares into swords, and your pruninghooks into spears: let the weak say, I *am* strong." Joel 3:10

July
14

_____
_____
_____
_____
_____
_____
_____
_____
_____
_____
_____
_____
_____
_____
_____
_____
_____
_____
_____
_____

"Thou hast made known to me the ways of life; thou shalt make me full of joy with thy countenance." Acts 2:28

July
15

_____

_____

_____

_____

_____

_____

_____

_____

_____

_____

_____

_____

_____

_____

_____

_____

_____

_____

_____

_____

_____

_____

"Hear, O Israel: The LORD our God *is* one LORD:"
Deuteronomy 6:4

July
16

"And they said, Believe on the Lord Jesus Christ, and thou shalt be saved, and thy house." Acts 16:31

July
17

"And thou shalt love the LORD thy God with all thine heart, and with all thy soul, and with all thy might." Deuteronomy 6:5

July
18

"I have shewed you all things, how that so labouring ye ought to support the weak, and to remember the words of the Lord Jesus, how he said, It is more blessed to give than to receive." Acts 20:35

July
19

"Be strong and of a good courage, fear not, nor be afraid of them: for the LORD thy God, he *it is* that doth go with thee; he will not fail thee, nor forsake thee."
Deuteronomy 31:6

July
20

"But the fruit of the Spirit is love, joy, peace, longsuffering, gentleness, goodness, faith," Galatians 5:22

July
21

"Let us hear the conclusion of the whole matter: Fear God, and keep his commandments: for this *is* the whole *duty* of man." Ecclesiastes 12:13

July
22

"Let not your heart be troubled: ye believe in God, believe also in me."
John 14:1

July
23

"Thou wilt keep *him* in perfect peace, *whose* mind *is* stayed *on thee*: because he trusteth in thee." Isaiah 26:3

July
24

July
25

"Trust ye in the LORD for ever: for in the LORD JEHOVAH
is everlasting strength:" Isaiah 26:4

July
26

_____

_____

_____

_____

_____

_____

_____

_____

_____

_____

_____

_____

_____

_____

_____

_____

_____

_____

_____

_____

"Jesus saith unto him, I am the way, the truth, and the life: no man cometh unto the Father, but by me." John 14:6

July
27

"He giveth power to the faint; and to *them that have* no might he increaseth strength."
Isaiah 40:29

July
28

July
29

"Fear thou not; for I *am* with thee: be not dismayed; for I *am* thy God: I will strengthen thee; yea, I will help thee; yea, I will uphold thee with the right hand of my righteousness." Isaiah 41:10

July
30

"But my God shall supply all your need according to his riches in glory by Christ Jesus." Phillippians 4:19

July
31

_____

_____

_____

_____

_____

_____

_____

_____

_____

_____

_____

_____

_____

_____

_____

_____

_____

_____

_____

_____

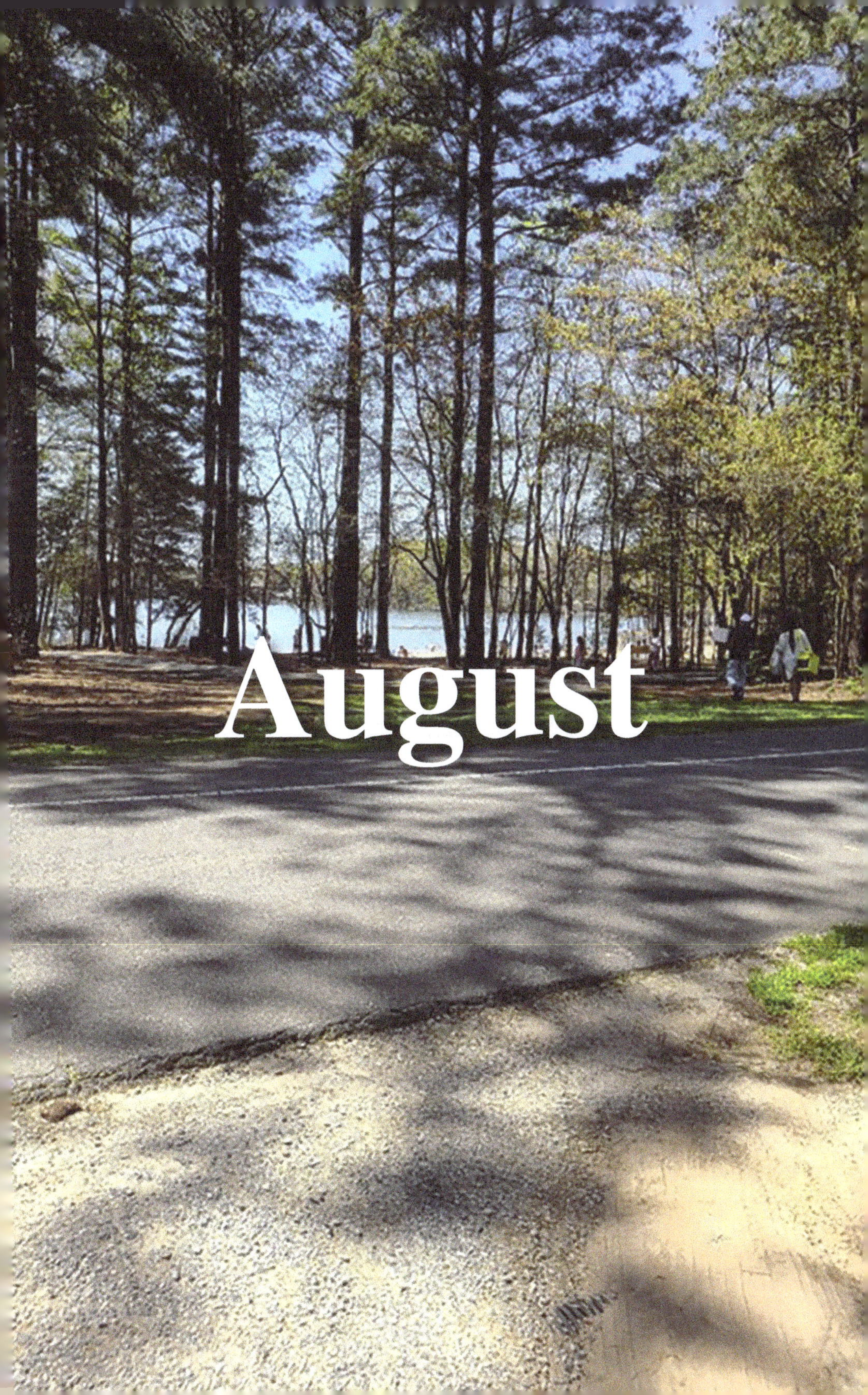
August

Above The Trees

When I look up toward the heavens
When I look beyond the trees,
The wonders of his beauty
Is all that I can see.

By the day I see the sunlight,
By the night I see the stars,
And through it all I realize,
How wonderful you are.

I thank you for the blessings,
That You upon me bestow,
And know that You are with me,
No matter where I go.

You taught me many lessons,
You brought me through much pain,
You were the light that showed the path,
To seek your face again.

And now that I have found You
I'll never turn away.
I'll read your word and sing your praise,
Each and every day!

"When thou passest through the waters, I *will be* with thee; and through the rivers, they shall not overflow thee: when thou walkest through the fire, thou shalt not be burned; neither shall the flame kindle upon thee."

August
1

_____

_____

_____

_____

_____

_____

_____

_____

_____

_____

_____

_____

_____

_____

_____

_____

_____

_____

August
2

_____

_____

_____

_____

_____

_____

_____

_____

_____

_____

_____

_____

_____

_____

_____

_____

_____

_____

_____

_____

"The grass withereth, the flower fadeth: but the word of our God shall stand for ever." Isaiah 40:8

August
3

_____

_____

_____

_____

_____

_____

_____

_____

_____

_____

_____

_____

_____

_____

_____

_____

_____

_____

_____

"Now the parable is this: The seed is the word of God."
Luke 8:11

August
4

_____

_____

_____

_____

_____

_____

_____

_____

_____

_____

_____

_____

_____

_____

_____

_____

_____

_____

_____

_____

_____

"I *am* the LORD, and *there is* none else, *there is* no God beside me:
I girded thee, though thou hast not known me:" Isaiah 45:5

August
5

_____

_____

_____

_____

_____

_____

_____

_____

_____

_____

_____

_____

_____

_____

_____

_____

_____

_____

_____

_____

"Jesus said unto him, If thou canst believe, all things *are* possible to him that believeth." Mark 9:23

August
6

_____

_____

_____

_____

_____

_____

_____

_____

_____

_____

_____

_____

_____

_____

_____

_____

_____

_____

_____

_____

_____

_____

"Look unto me, and be ye saved, all the ends of the earth: for I *am* God, and *there is* none else." Isaiah 45:22

August
7

_____

_____

_____

_____

_____

_____

_____

_____

_____

_____

_____

_____

_____

_____

_____

_____

_____

_____

_____

_____

"And Jesus answering saith unto them, Have faith in God." Mark 11:22

August
8

_____

_____

_____

_____

_____

_____

_____

_____

_____

_____

_____

_____

_____

_____

_____

_____

_____

_____

_____

_____

_____

_____

"Seek ye the LORD while he may be found, call ye upon him while he is near:" Isaiah 55:6

August
9

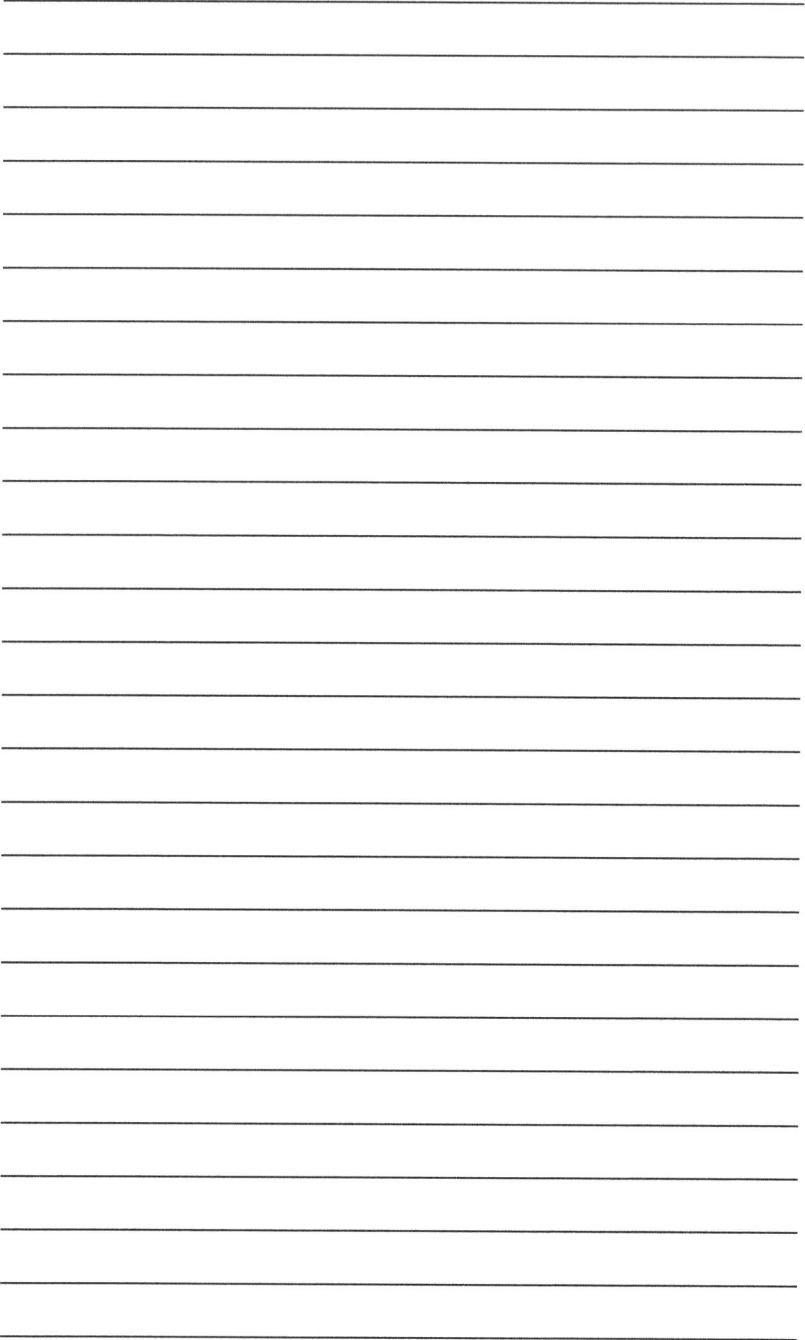

August
10

_____

_____

_____

_____

_____

_____

_____

_____

_____

_____

_____

_____

_____

_____

_____

_____

_____

_____

_____

_____

_____

_____

"They bear him upon the shoulder, they carry him, and set him in his place, and he standeth; from his place shall he not remove: yea, *one* shall cry unto him, yet can he not answer, nor save him out of his trouble."
Isaiah 46:7

August
11

"For many shall come in my name, saying, I am *Christ*; and shall deceive many." Mark 13:6

August
12

_____

_____

_____

_____

_____

_____

_____

_____

_____

_____

_____

_____

_____

_____

_____

_____

_____

_____

_____

_____

_____

_____

_____

"Arise, shine; for thy light is come, and the glory of the LORD is risen upon thee." Isaiah 60:1

August
13

August 14

"Blessed *is* the man that trusteth in the LORD, and whose hope the LORD is." Jeremiah 17:7

August
15

"Blessed *are* they that mourn: for they shall be comforted."
Matthew 5:4

August
16

"Heal me, O LORD, and I shall be healed; save me, and
I shall be saved: for thou *art* my praise." Jeremiah 17:14

August
17

_____

_____

_____

_____

_____

_____

_____

_____

_____

_____

_____

_____

_____

_____

_____

_____

_____

_____

"Blessed *are* the meek: for they shall inherit the earth."
Matthew 5:5

August
18

_____

_____

_____

_____

_____

_____

_____

_____

_____

_____

_____

_____

_____

_____

_____

_____

_____

_____

_____

_____

_____

_____

_____

_____

"For I know the thoughts that I think toward you, saith the LORD, thoughts of peace, and not of evil, to give you an expected end." Jeremiah 29:11

August
19

August
20

_____

_____

_____

_____

_____

_____

_____

_____

_____

_____

_____

_____

_____

_____

_____

_____

_____

_____

_____

_____

_____

"Thus speaketh the Lord God of Israel, saying, Write thee all the words that I have spoken unto thee in a book." Jeremiah 30:2

August
21

_____

_____

_____

_____

_____

_____

_____

_____

_____

_____

_____

_____

_____

_____

_____

_____

_____

_____

_____

_____

_____

_____

"Blessed *are* the merciful: for they shall obtain mercy."
Matthew 5:7

August
22

"Then shall ye call upon me, and ye shall go and pray unto me, and I will hearken unto you." Jeremiah 29:12

August
23

August
24

_____

_____

_____

_____

_____

_____

_____

_____

_____

_____

_____

_____

_____

_____

_____

_____

_____

_____

_____

_____

_____

_____

_____

_____

"And ye shall seek me, and find me, when ye shall search for me with all your heart." Jeremiah 29:13

August
25

August
26

_____

_____

_____

_____

_____

_____

_____

_____

_____

_____

_____

_____

_____

_____

_____

_____

_____

_____

_____

"For I will restore health unto thee, and I will heal thee of thy
wounds, saith the LORD; because they called thee an Outcast,
saying, This is Zion, whom no man seeketh after." Jeremiah 30:17

August
27

_____

_____

_____

_____

_____

_____

_____

_____

_____

_____

_____

_____

_____

_____

_____

_____

_____

_____

"Blessed *are* they which are persecuted for righteousness' sake: for theirs is the kingdom of heaven." Matthew 5:10

August
28

"God is jealous, and the LORD revengeth; the LORD revengeth, and is furious; the LORD will take vengeance his adversaries, and he reserveth wrath for his enemies." Nahum 1:2

August
29

"Blessed are ye, when *men* shall revile you, and persecute *you*,
and shall say all manner of evil against you falsely, for my sake."
Matthew 5:11

August
30

"The LORD is slow to anger, and great in power, and will not at all acquit the wicked: the LORD hath his way in the whirlwind and in the storm, and the clouds are the dust of his feet." Nahum 1:3

August 31

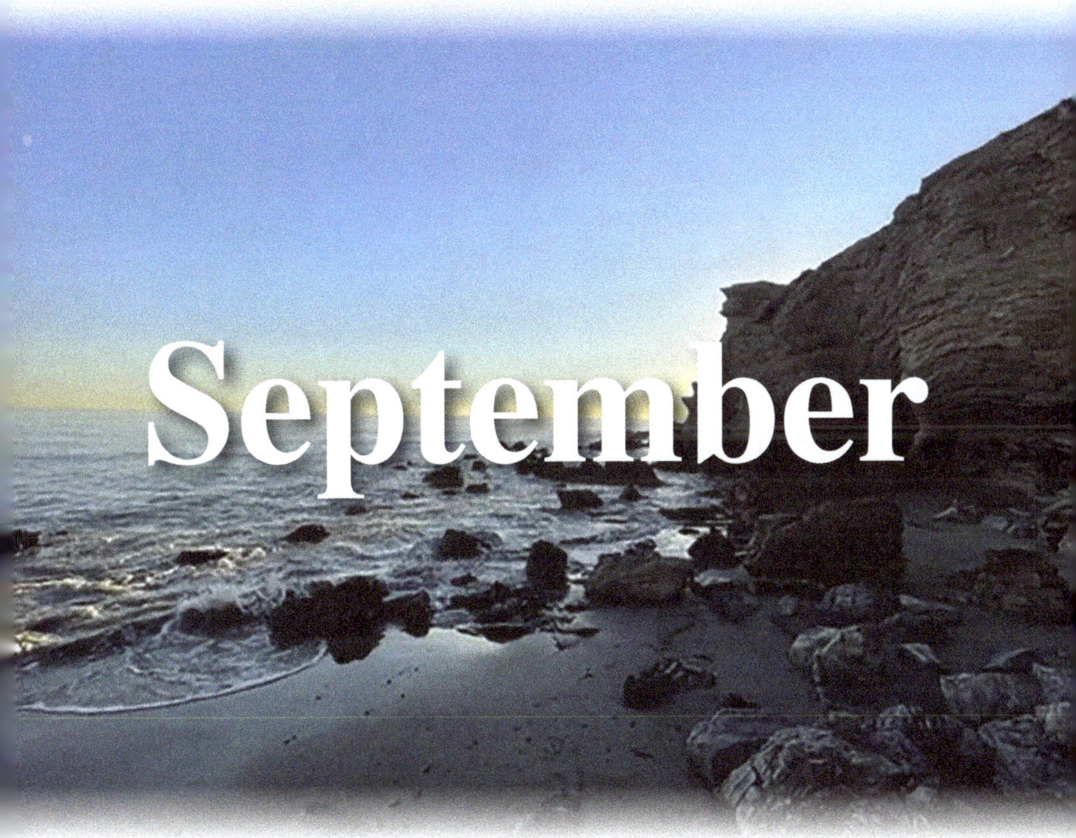
September

Seasons

As the sun sets early, and the clouds roll in,
These are all signs that winter begins,
The air turns chilly as the temperature drops,
And the birds no longer sing perched in the tree tops.

This, is one of the seasons out of the four,
Some people like less, some people like more,
I am thankful I get to see them all,
And I know that each new day I see,
Is based on the Master's call.

I thank Him each day when I awake,
For the strength to get me through,
And no matter what this day may bring,
God I know, it's me and You!

"Let your light so shine before men, that they may see your good works, and glorify your Father which is in heaven." Matthew 5:16

September
1

_____

_____

_____

_____

_____

_____

_____

_____

_____

_____

_____

_____

_____

_____

_____

_____

_____

_____

_____

_____

_____

_____

"The LORD is good, a strong hold in the day of trouble; and he knoweth them that trust in him." Nahim 1:7

September
2

_____

_____

_____

_____

_____

_____

_____

_____

_____

_____

_____

_____

_____

_____

_____

_____

_____

_____

_____

_____

_____

_____

_____

_____

"Rejoice, and be exceeding glad: for great is your reward in heaven:
for so persecuted they the prophets which were before you."
Matthew 5:12

September
3

_____

_____

_____

_____

_____

_____

_____

_____

_____

_____

_____

_____

_____

_____

_____

_____

_____

_____

_____

"And it shall come to pass, that whosoever shall call on the name of the LORD shall be delivered: for in mount Zion and in Jerusalem shall be deliverance, as the LORD hath said, and in the remnant whom the LORD shall call." Joel 2:32

September
4

"Ye are the salt of the earth: but if the salt have lost his savour, wherewith shall it be salted? it is thenceforth good for nothing, but to be cast out, and to be trodden under foot of men." Matthew 5:13

September
5

_____

_____

_____

_____

_____

_____

_____

_____

_____

_____

_____

_____

_____

_____

_____

_____

_____

_____

_____

_____

"It is of the LORD's mercies that we are not consumed, because his compassions fail not." Lamentations 3:22

September
6

"Ye are the light of the world. A city that is set on a hill cannot be hid."
Matthew 5:14

September
7

"They are new every morning: great is thy faithfulness."
Lamentations 3:23

September
8

_____

_____

_____

_____

_____

_____

_____

_____

_____

_____

_____

_____

_____

_____

_____

_____

_____

_____

_____

"Neither do men light a candle, and put it under a bushel, but on a candlestick; and it giveth light unto all that are in the house."
Matthew 5:15

September
9

"The LORD is my portion, saith my soul; therefore will I hope in him."
Lamentations 3:24

September
10

"Ask, and it shall be given you; seek, and ye shall find; knock, and
it shall be opened unto you:" Matthew 7:7

September
11

_____

_____

_____

_____

_____

_____

_____

_____

_____

_____

_____

_____

_____

_____

_____

_____

_____

_____

_____

_____

_____

_____

"The Lord is good unto them that wait for him, to the soul that seeketh him." Lamentations 3:25

September
12

_____

_____

_____

_____

_____

_____

_____

_____

_____

_____

_____

_____

_____

_____

_____

_____

_____

_____

_____

_____

_____

"Come unto me, all ye that labour and are heavy laden, and I will give you rest." Matthew 11:28

September
13

"It is good that a man should both hope and quietly wait for the salvation of the LORD." Lamentations 3:26

September 14

_____

_____

_____

_____

_____

_____

_____

_____

_____

_____

_____

_____

_____

_____

_____

_____

_____

_____

_____

_____

"Take my yoke upon you, and learn of me; for I am meek and lowly
in heart: and ye shall find rest unto your souls." Matthew 11:29

September 15

"Then he said unto them, Go your way, eat the fat, and drink the sweet, and send portions unto them for whom nothing is prepared: for this day is holy unto our LORD: neither be ye sorry; for the joy of the LORD is your strength." Nehemiah 8:10

September
16

"For my yoke is easy, and my burden is light." Matthew 11:30

September
17

_____

_____

_____

_____

_____

_____

_____

_____

_____

_____

_____

_____

_____

_____

_____

_____

_____

_____

_____

_____

_____

"The Lord bless thee, and keep thee: The LORD make his face shine upon thee, and be gracious unto thee:" Numbers 6:24-25

September 18

_____

_____

_____

_____

_____

_____

_____

_____

_____

_____

_____

_____

_____

_____

_____

_____

_____

_____

_____

_____

"And all things, whatsoever ye shall ask in prayer, believing, ye shall receive." Matthew 21:22

September
19

"The LORD lift up his countenance upon thee, and give thee peace."
Numbers 6:26

September
20

"Be watchful, and strengthen the things which remain, that are ready to die: for I have not found thy works perfect before God." Revelation 3:2

September
21

"He keepeth the paths of judgment, and preserveth the way of his saints."
Proverbs 2:8

September
22

_____

_____

_____

_____

_____

_____

_____

_____

_____

_____

_____

_____

_____

_____

_____

_____

_____

_____

_____

_____

_____

"Behold, I stand at the door, and knock: if any man hear my voice, and open the door, I will come in to him, and will sup with him, and he with me."
Revelation 3:20

September
23

_____

_____

_____

_____

_____

_____

_____

_____

_____

_____

_____

_____

_____

_____

_____

_____

_____

_____

_____

_____

_____

"For we are the circumcision, which worship God in the spirit, and
rejoice in Christ Jesus, and have no confidence in the flesh."
Philippians 3:3

September 24

"Discretion shall preserve thee, understanding shall keep thee:"
Proverbs 2:11

September
25

_____

_____

_____

_____

_____

_____

_____

_____

_____

_____

_____

_____

_____

_____

_____

_____

_____

_____

_____

_____

_____

_____

"Therefore we ought to give the more earnest heed to the things which we have heard, lest at any time we should let them slip." Hebrews 2:1

September 26

"If thou seekest her as silver, and searchest for her as for hid treasures;"
Proverbs 2:4

September
27

_____

_____

_____

_____

_____

_____

_____

_____

_____

_____

_____

_____

_____

_____

_____

_____

_____

_____

_____

_____

"How shall we escape, if we neglect so great salvation; which at the first began to be spoken by the Lord, and was confirmed unto us by them that heard him;" Hebrews 2:3

September
28

_____

_____

_____

_____

_____

_____

_____

_____

_____

_____

_____

_____

_____

_____

_____

_____

_____

_____

_____

"Hear, ye children, the instruction of a father, and attend to know understanding." Proverbs 4:1

September 29

"God also bearing them witness, both with signs and wonders, and with divers miracles, and gifts of the Holy Ghost, according to his own will? Hebrews 2:4

September
30

October

The Autumn Leaves

I sit and watch the Autumn leaves
Change colors every day,
I'll look again this time next month,
And they'll all be blown away.

They are so beautiful today
Shades of yellow, orange, and brown
But then I"ll look again next month,
And they'll all be on the ground.

But I know they'll come back next spring
The way they always do,
And I'll look up toward heaven and say
Dear Lord, its all thanks to you!

"He layeth up sound wisdom for the righteous: he is a buckler to them that walk uprightly." Proverbs 2:7

October
1

"And what is the exceeding greatness of his power to us-ward who believe, according to the working of his mighty power,"
Ephesians 1:19

October
2

_____

_____

_____

_____

_____

_____

_____

_____

_____

_____

_____

_____

_____

_____

_____

_____

_____

_____

_____

_____

"He taught me also, and said unto me, Let thine heart retain my words: keep my commandments, and live." Proverbs 4:4

October
3

"He that overcometh shall inherit all things; and I will be his God, and he shall be my son." Revelation 21:7

October
4

_____

_____

_____

_____

_____

_____

_____

_____

_____

_____

_____

_____

_____

_____

_____

_____

_____

_____

_____

_____

_____

_____

"Which he wrought in Christ, when he raised him from the dead, and set
him at his own right hand in the heavenly places" Ephesians 1:20

October
5

"He taught me also, and said unto me, Let thine heart retain my words: keep my commandments, and live." Proverbs 4:4

October
6

"Far above all principality, and power, and might, and dominion, and
every name that is named, not only in this world, but also in that which
is to come:" Ephesians 1:21

October
7

_____

_____

_____

_____

_____

_____

_____

_____

_____

_____

_____

_____

_____

_____

_____

_____

_____

_____

"Get wisdom, get understanding: forget it not; neither decline from the words of my mouth." Proverbs 4:5

October
8

"Unto me, who am less than the least of all saints, is this grace given, that I should preach among the Gentiles the unsearchable riches of Christ;"
Ephesians 3:8

October
9

"I have taught thee in the way of wisdom; I have led thee in right paths."
Proverbs 4:11

October
10

"For this cause I bow my knees unto the Father of our Lord Jesus Christ,"
Ephesians 3:14

October
11

"But the path of the just is as the shining light, that shineth more and more unto the perfect day." Proverbs 4:18

October
12

_____

_____

_____

_____

_____

_____

_____

_____

_____

_____

_____

_____

_____

_____

_____

_____

_____

_____

_____

_____

"That he would grant you, according to the riches of his glory, to be strengthened with might by his Spirit in the inner man;"
Ephesians 3:16

October
13

_____

_____

_____

_____

_____

_____

_____

_____

_____

_____

_____

_____

_____

_____

_____

_____

_____

_____

_____

_____

"My son, attend to my words; incline thine ear unto my sayings."
Proverbs 4:20

October
14

_____

_____

_____

_____

_____

_____

_____

_____

_____

_____

_____

_____

_____

_____

_____

_____

_____

_____

_____

_____

"That Christ may dwell in your hearts by faith; that ye, being rooted and grounded in love," Ephesians 3:17

October
15

_____

_____

_____

_____

_____

_____

_____

_____

_____

_____

_____

_____

_____

_____

_____

_____

_____

_____

_____

"Keep thy heart with all diligence; for out of it are the issues of life."
Proverbs 4:23

October
16

_____
_____
_____
_____
_____
_____
_____
_____
_____
_____
_____
_____
_____
_____
_____
_____
_____
_____
_____
_____
_____

"And to know the love of Christ, which passeth knowledge, that ye might be filled with all the fulness of God." Ephesians 3:19

October
17

"Turn not to the right hand nor to the left: remove thy foot from evil."
Proverbs 4:27

October
18

_____

_____

_____

_____

_____

_____

_____

_____

_____

_____

_____

_____

_____

_____

_____

_____

_____

_____

"For I long to see you, that I may impart unto you some spiritual gift,
to the end ye may be established." Romans 1:11

October
19

_____

_____

_____

_____

_____

_____

_____

_____

_____

_____

_____

_____

_____

_____

_____

_____

_____

_____

_____

_____

"Commit thy works unto the LORD, and thy thoughts shall be established."
Proverbs 16:3

October
20

"That is, that I may be comforted together with you by the mutual faith both of you and me." Romans 1:12

October
21

_____

_____

_____

_____

_____

_____

_____

_____

_____

_____

_____

_____

_____

_____

_____

_____

_____

_____

_____

_____

_____

_____

"My son, keep my words, and lay up my commandments with thee."
Proverbs 7:1

October
22

"Therefore being justified by faith, we have peace with God through
our Lord Jesus Christ:" Romans 5:1

October
23

_____

_____

_____

_____

_____

_____

_____

_____

_____

_____

_____

_____

_____

_____

_____

_____

_____

_____

_____

_____

_____

"Counsel is mine, and sound wisdom: I am understanding; I have strength."
Proverbs 8:14

October
24

"Therefore being justified by faith, we have peace with God through our Lord Jesus Christ:" Romans 5:3

October
25

_____

_____

_____

_____

_____

_____

_____

_____

_____

_____

_____

_____

_____

_____

_____

_____

_____

_____

_____

_____

_____

_____

"Now therefore hearken unto me, O ye children: for blessed are they that keep my ways." Proverbs 8:32

October
26

_____

_____

_____

_____

_____

_____

_____

_____

_____

_____

_____

_____

_____

_____

_____

_____

_____

_____

_____

_____

_____

"And not only so, but we glory in tribulations also: knowing that tribulation worketh patience;" Romans 5:3

October
27

_____

_____

_____

_____

_____

_____

_____

_____

_____

_____

_____

_____

_____

_____

_____

_____

_____

_____

_____

_____

"For whoso findeth me findeth life, and shall obtain favour of the LORD."
Proverbs 8:35

October
28

"But God commendeth his love toward us, in that, while we were yet sinners, Christ died for us." Romans 5:8

October 29

"The fear of the LORD is the beginning of wisdom: and the knowledge of the holy is understanding." Proverbs 9:10

October
30

_____

_____

_____

_____

_____

_____

_____

_____

_____

_____

_____

_____

_____

_____

_____

_____

_____

_____

"For as many as are led by the Spirit of God, they are the sons of God."
Romans 8:14

October
31

_____

_____

_____

_____

_____

_____

_____

_____

_____

_____

_____

_____

_____

_____

_____

_____

_____

_____

_____

_____

_____

_____

_____

November

Grateful

Did you ever take time to think about
What you should be grateful for?
What the heavenly Father has done for you
And the things we tend to ignore.

The things we take for granted
As we go through each day,
Sometimes we seem too busy
To even stop and pray.

We're rushing here, and rushing there
Busy schedules trying to keep,
We need our eyes to see our way,
For our balance we need our feet.

We have so many attributes
That we use everyday,
So don't tell me you don't have time
To raise your hands and pray.

I could list at least twenty things
You should be grateful for,
So lets just use one, and raise our voice
In praise to our almighty Lord.

"He that handleth a matter wisely shall find good: and whoso
trusteth in the LORD, happy *is* he." Proverbs 16:20

November
1

_____

_____

_____

_____

_____

_____

_____

_____

_____

_____

_____

_____

_____

_____

_____

_____

_____

_____

_____

"The Spirit itself beareth witness with our spirit, that we are the children of God:" Romans 8:16

November
2

_____

_____

_____

_____

_____

_____

_____

_____

_____

_____

_____

_____

_____

_____

_____

_____

_____

_____

_____

_____

_____

_____

_____

"A merry heart doeth good *like* a medicine: but a broken spirit drieth the bones." Proverbs 17:22

November
3

_____

_____

_____

_____

_____

_____

_____

_____

_____

_____

_____

_____

_____

_____

_____

_____

_____

_____

_____

_____

"And we know that all things work together for good to them that love
God, to them who are the called according to *his* purpose."
Romans 8:28

November
4

"The name of the LORD *is* a strong tower: the righteous runneth into it, and is safe." Proverbs 18:10

November
5

_____

_____

_____

_____

_____

_____

_____

_____

_____

_____

_____

_____

_____

_____

_____

_____

_____

_____

_____

_____

_____

"Nay, in all these things we are more than conquerors through him that loved us." Romans 8:37

November
6

_____

_____

_____

_____

_____

_____

_____

_____

_____

_____

_____

_____

_____

_____

_____

_____

_____

_____

_____

_____

_____

"Death and life are in the power of the tongue: and they that love it shall eat the fruit thereof." Proverbs 18:21

November
7

_____

_____

_____

_____

_____

_____

_____

_____

_____

_____

_____

_____

_____

_____

_____

_____

_____

_____

_____

_____

_____

_____

"For I am persuaded, that neither death, nor life, nor angels, nor principalities, nor powers, nor things present, nor things to come," Romans 8:38

November
8

_____

_____

_____

_____

_____

_____

_____

_____

_____

_____

_____

_____

_____

_____

_____

_____

_____

_____

_____

"Apply thine heart unto instruction, and thine ears to the words of knowledge." Proverbs 23:12

November
9

_____

_____

_____

_____

_____

_____

_____

_____

_____

_____

_____

_____

_____

_____

_____

_____

_____

_____

_____

"Nor height, nor depth, nor any other creature, shall be able to separate us from the love of God, which is in Christ Jesus our Lord." Romans 8:39

November
10

"Hear thou, my son, and be wise, and guide thine heart in the way."
Proverbs 23:19

November
11

"Let love be without dissimulation. Abhor that which is evil; cleave to that which is good." Romans 12:9

November 12

"Buy the truth, and sell it not; also wisdom, and instruction, and understanding." Proverbs 23:23

November
13

_____

_____

_____

_____

_____

_____

_____

_____

_____

_____

_____

_____

_____

_____

_____

_____

_____

_____

_____

_____

"Rejoicing in hope; patient in tribulation; continuing instant in prayer;"
Romans 12:12

November
14

_____

_____

_____

_____

_____

_____

_____

_____

_____

_____

_____

_____

_____

_____

_____

_____

_____

_____

_____

"My son, give me thine heart, and let thine eyes observe my ways."
Proverbs 23:26

November
15

_____

_____

_____

_____

_____

_____

_____

_____

_____

_____

_____

_____

_____

_____

_____

_____

_____

_____

_____

_____

_____

"If it be possible, as much as lieth in you, live peaceably with all men."
Romans 12:18

November
16

_____

_____

_____

_____

_____

_____

_____

_____

_____

_____

_____

_____

_____

_____

_____

_____

_____

_____

_____

_____

"Blessed are they that keep his testimonies, and that seek him with the whole heart." Psalm 119:2

November
17

"Be not overcome of evil, but overcome evil with good." Romans 12:21

November
18

_____

_____

_____

_____

_____

_____

_____

_____

_____

_____

_____

_____

_____

_____

_____

_____

_____

_____

_____

"I will delight myself in thy statutes: I will not forget thy word."
Psalm 119:16

November 19

_____
_____
_____
_____
_____
_____
_____
_____
_____
_____
_____
_____
_____
_____
_____
_____
_____
_____
_____
_____
_____
_____

"For Christ is the end of the law for righteousness to every one that believeth." Romans 10:4

November
20

_____

_____

_____

_____

_____

_____

_____

_____

_____

_____

_____

_____

_____

_____

_____

_____

_____

_____

_____

_____

_____

"Be wise now therefore, O ye kings: be instructed, ye judges of the earth." Psalm 2:10

November
21

_____

_____

_____

_____

_____

_____

_____

_____

_____

_____

_____

_____

_____

_____

_____

_____

_____

_____

_____

_____

_____

"For the scripture saith, Whosoever believeth on him shall not be ashamed." Romans 10:11

November 22

"He loveth righteousness and judgment: the earth is full of the goodness of the LORD." Psalm 33:5

November
23

"But is now made manifest by the appearing of our Saviour Jesus Christ, who hath abolished death, and hath brought life and immortality to light through the gospel:" 2 Timothy 1:10

November
24

"The words of his mouth are iniquity and deceit: he hath left off to be wise, and to do good." Psalm 36:3

November
25

_____

_____

_____

_____

_____

_____

_____

_____

_____

_____

_____

_____

_____

_____

_____

_____

_____

_____

_____

_____

_____

_____

_____

_____

"If a man therefore purge himself from these, he shall be a vessel unto honour, sanctified, and meet for the master's use, and prepared unto every good work."
2 Timothy 2:21

November
26

"For a just man falleth seven times, and riseth up again: but the wicked shall fall into mischief." Proverbs 24:16

November
27

_____
_____
_____
_____
_____
_____
_____
_____
_____
_____
_____
_____
_____
_____
_____
_____
_____
_____
_____
_____

"Let every soul be subject unto the higher powers. For there is
no power but of God: the powers that be are ordained of God."
Romans 13:1

November
28

_____

_____

_____

_____

_____

_____

_____

_____

_____

_____

_____

_____

_____

_____

_____

_____

_____

_____

"When a man's ways please the LORD, he maketh even his enemies to be at peace with him." Proverbs 16:7

November 29

"For by grace are ye saved through faith; and that not of yourselves:
it is the gift of God:" Ephesians 2:8

November
30

_____

_____

_____

_____

_____

_____

_____

_____

_____

_____

_____

_____

_____

_____

_____

_____

_____

_____

_____

_____

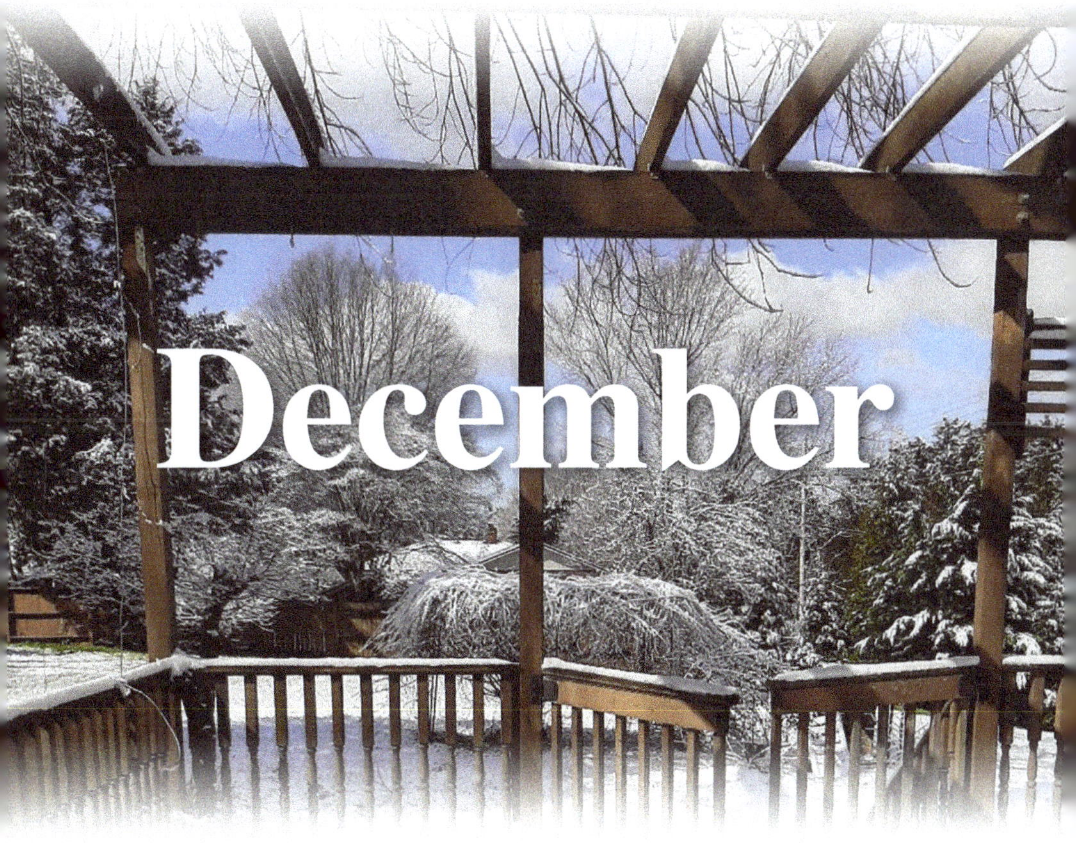
December

The Greatest Story Ever Told

Three wise men came from afar,
They were led there only by a star
The star led to a stable in Bethlehem,
And they brought Gold, Frankincense
and Myrrh with them.
They said he was the child they were to behold
And thus began the greatest story ever told.

As Jesus grew older, and matured into a man
That's when the challenges of his endurance began,
There were many obstacles with which he did contend
Of trials and tribulations for him, there seemed no end.

Yes, he did many miracles, and did them all the time
He made the lame to walk, raised the dead,
Cured the sick, and healed the blind.

He had twelve men travelling with him
Disciples they were called,
But they were more than just mere men,
They were servants of the Lord.

The people came from far and wide
Just to hear his word,
They were enthralled and mesmerized,
By everything they heard.

They praised him and adored him
And claimed him King of Kings,
For truly they had never seen
Such monumental things.

But there were Priests and Rabbis
who didn't understand
How he could do such miracles
by the movement of his hand,
They called him blasphemer, magician, and a fake
They did not know, he was doing this for His
Father's sake.

They had him bound and shackled,
A crown of thorns upon his head
And then they nailed him to the cross,
And left him there til dead.

Our Jesus died for all our sins
Of that you can be sure,
Don't ever lose sight of that fact
Give him praise forever more.

And with your praise
Keep this in mind,
Jesus said I'm with you
Every day till the end of time.

"Be not a witness against thy neighbour without cause; and deceive not
[with thy lips." Proverbs 24:28

December
1

_____

_____

_____

_____

_____

_____

_____

_____

_____

_____

_____

_____

_____

_____

_____

_____

_____

_____

_____

_____

_____

_____

_____

"Verily, verily, I say unto you, He that entereth not by the door into the sheepfold, but climbeth up some other way, the same is a thief and a robber." John 10:1

December
2

_____

_____

_____

_____

_____

_____

_____

_____

_____

_____

_____

_____

_____

_____

_____

_____

_____

_____

_____

"In thee, O LORD, do I put my trust; let me never be ashamed: deliver me in thy righteousness." Psalm 31:1

December
3

_____

_____

_____

_____

_____

_____

_____

_____

_____

_____

_____

_____

_____

_____

_____

_____

_____

_____

_____

_____

_____

_____

"See then that ye walk circumspectly, not as fools, but as wise,"
Ephesians 5:15

December

4

_____

_____

_____

_____

_____

_____

_____

_____

_____

_____

_____

_____

_____

_____

_____

_____

_____

_____

_____

_____

_____

_____

"But they that wait upon the Lord shall renew their strength; they shall mount up with wings as eagles; they shall run, and not be weary; and they shall walk and not faint." Isaiah 40:31

December
5

_____

_____

_____

_____

_____

_____

_____

_____

_____

_____

_____

_____

_____

_____

_____

_____

_____

_____

_____

_____

[16] "Redeeming the time, because the days are evil. [17] Wherefore be ye not unwise, but understanding what the will of the Lord is." Ephesians 5:16-17

December
6

"I, even I, am the Lord; and beside me there is no saviour" Isaiah 43:11

December
7

"And be not drunk with wine, wherein is excess; but be filled with the Spirit;"
Ephesians 5:18

December
8

_____

_____

_____

_____

_____

_____

_____

_____

_____

_____

_____

_____

_____

_____

_____

_____

_____

_____

_____

_____

_____

"The LORD shall fight for you, and ye shall hold your peace."
Exodus 14:14

December
9

_____

_____

_____

_____

_____

_____

_____

_____

_____

_____

_____

_____

_____

_____

_____

_____

_____

_____

_____

_____

_____

_____

_____

_____

_____

_____

_____

"Speaking to yourselves in psalms and hymns and spiritual songs, singing and making melody in your heart to the Lord;"
Ephesians 5:19

December
10

"For I am the Lord, I change not; therefore ye sons of Jacob are not consumed." Malachi 3:6

December 11

_____

_____

_____

_____

_____

_____

_____

_____

_____

_____

_____

_____

_____

_____

_____

_____

_____

_____

_____

_____

_____

_____

"Giving thanks always for all things unto God and the Father in the name of our Lord Jesus Christ;" Ephesians 5:20

December
12

"Cast thy burden upon the LORD, and he shall sustain thee:
he shall never suffer the righteous to be moved." Psalm 55:22

December
13

"But the Lord is faithful, who shall stablish you, and keep you from evil." 2 Thessalonians 3:3

December
14

_____

_____

_____

_____

_____

_____

_____

_____

_____

_____

_____

_____

_____

_____

_____

_____

_____

_____

_____

_____

"Though thou exalt thyself as the eagle, and though thou set thy
nest among the stars, thence will I bring thee down, saith the LORD."
Obadiah 1:4

December
15

"And the Lord direct your hearts into the love of God, and into the patient waiting for Christ." 2 Thessalonians 3:5

December
16

_____

_____

_____

_____

_____

_____

_____

_____

_____

_____

_____

_____

_____

_____

_____

_____

_____

_____

_____

"And the angel of the Lord appeared unto him, and said unto him,
The Lord is with thee, thou mighty man of valour." Judges 6:12

December
17

_____

_____

_____

_____

_____

_____

_____

_____

_____

_____

_____

_____

_____

_____

_____

_____

_____

_____

_____

_____

"For there is one God, and one mediator between God
and men, the man Christ Jesus;" 1 Timothy 2:5

December
18

"The LORD hath appeared of old unto me, saying, Yea,
I have loved thee with an everlasting love : therefore with
lovingkindness have I drawn thee." Jeremiah 31:3

December 19

_____

_____

_____

_____

_____

_____

_____

_____

_____

_____

_____

_____

_____

_____

_____

_____

_____

_____

"It is a faithful saying: For if we be dead with him, we shall also live with him:" 2 Timothy 2:11

December
20

_____

_____

_____

_____

_____

_____

_____

_____

_____

_____

_____

_____

_____

_____

_____

_____

_____

_____

_____

_____

_____

"I have set the LORD always before me: because he is at my right hand,
I shall not be moved." Psalm 16:8

December
21

_____

_____

_____

_____

_____

_____

_____

_____

_____

_____

_____

_____

_____

_____

_____

_____

_____

_____

_____

_____

_____

_____

_____

_____

"For unto you is born this day in the city of David a Saviour,
which is Christ the Lord." Luke 2:11

December
22

_____

_____

_____

_____

_____

_____

_____

_____

_____

_____

_____

_____

_____

_____

_____

_____

_____

_____

_____

_____

"For unto us a child is born, unto us a son is given: and the government shall be upon his shoulder: and his name shall be called Wonderful, Counsellor, The mighty God, The everlasting Father, The Prince of Peace." Isaiah 9:6

December 23

"And this shall be a sign unto you; Ye shall find the babe wrapped in swaddling clothes, lying in a manger." Luke 2:12

December
24

"But he was wounded for our transgressions, he was bruised for our iniquities: the chastisement of our peace was upon him; and with his stripes we are healed." Isaiah 53:5

December
25

"And Jesus increased in wisdom and stature, and in favour
with God and man." Luke 2:52

December
26

_____

_____

_____

_____

_____

_____

_____

_____

_____

_____

_____

_____

_____

_____

_____

_____

_____

_____

_____

_____

_____

"All we like sheep have gone astray; we have turned every one
to his own way; and the LORD hath laid on him the iniquity of
us all." Isaiah 53:6

December
27

"Now unto him that is able to keep you from falling, and to present you faultless before the presence of his glory with exceeding joy,"
Jude 24

December
28

_____

_____

_____

_____

_____

_____

_____

_____

_____

_____

_____

_____

_____

_____

_____

_____

_____

_____

_____

_____

_____

"He was oppressed, and he was afflicted, yet he opened not his mouth: he is brought as a lamb to the slaughter, and as a sheep before her shearers is dumb, so he openeth not his mouth."
Isaiah 53:7

December
29

"To the only wise God our Saviour, be glory and majesty, dominion and power, both now and ever. Amen." Jude 25

December
30

"I will extol thee, my God, O king; and I will bless thy name for ever and ever." Psalm 145:1

December
31

_____

_____

_____

_____

_____

_____

_____

_____

_____

_____

_____

_____

_____

_____

_____

_____

_____

_____

_____

_____

_____

_____

_____

ABOUT THE AUTHORS

Lelia L. Lewis is a retired financial specialist, with a God-given gift for poetry.

She received her education through the Philadelphia Public School System, and attended Temple Preparatory School followed by Business School.

She entered the media world as a news castor for WDAS Radio, and then progressed to hosting a Gospel Cable TV Show in Delaware and Pennsylvania. She began hosting numerous Gospel programs in the Tri- state area and became a member of a gospel female quartet.

After several years, she went into the financial industry. There she became licensed in Auto, Home, Life, Health, and Mutual Funds. She spent the next twenty years servicing others in those areas.

She said "Poetry was always in my mind, but after retirement I had time to focus on it."

As I read the Bible more, I began to write poetry about what I read and felt. Now, I want share it with others in hopes that they will get some encouragement from my words, and find the joy in reading them that I find in writing them.

759

Rev. Denise Marshall is a passionate preacher and writer. She is the Founder of Word in Script Educational Ministries where she shares the full expression of her giftings with the community.

She was educated in the Philadelphia Public and Parochial School Systems. She has received a Bachelor of Arts Degree in Biblical Theology, as well as a Bachelor of Science Degree in Nursing, and is currently completing studies for a Master of Divinity Degree at Hood Theological Seminary.

Rev. Marshall has dedicated her life to the Lord and serves with joy in pastoral duties at her home church and in the community. She facilitates the Sunday evening Family & Friends Power Prayer Conference Call, also the monthly Word in Script Worldwide Book Review, and quarterly Author's Guild.

Her daily life consists of being a wife, mother, grandmother and great-grandmother to her family, as well as a CNA Instructor, Health & Wellness Advocate and Transformative Nurse Coach.

Even with a full and busy life, she is adamant about taking time to pray, read the Word and write. She is certain that God has blessed and gifted her abundantly to give to and help others. So it is with great pleasure and thankfulness that she seeks to serve in Kingdom Building by sharing the gospel in written poetic form.